CALUMET CITY PUBLIC LIBRARY

3 1613 00510 8074

S0-BJA-038

91.06
OH

Water Parks

By Virginia Loh-Hagan

CALUMET CITY PUBLIC LIBRARY

21st Century
Junior Library

Published in the United States of America by
Cherry Lake Publishing
Ann Arbor, Michigan
www.cherrylakepublishing.com

Content Adviser: Dr. Todd Kelley, Associate Professor of Engineering/Technology Teacher Education, Purdue Polytechnic Institute, West Lafayette, Indiana
Reading Adviser: Marla Conn MS, Ed., Literacy specialist, Read-Ability, Inc.

Photo Credits: © ESOlex/Shutterstock Images, cover; © VaLiza/Shutterstock Images, 4; © Per Andersen/Alamy Stock Photo, 6; © Shestakoff/Shutterstock Images, 8; © Oleksiy Maksymenko Photography/Alamy Stock Photo, 10; © Ruta Production/Shutterstock Images, 12; © pukkhoom_nokwila/Shutterstock Images, 14; © Brocreative/Shutterstock Images, 16; © Martin Valigursky/Shutterstock Images, 18

Copyright © 2017 by Cherry Lake Publishing
All rights reserved. No part of this book may be reproduced or utilized in any
form or by any means without written permission from the publisher.

Library of Congress Cataloging-in-Publication data on file.

Cherry Lake Publishing would like to acknowledge the work of The Partnership for 21st Century Learning.
Please visit *www.p21.org* for more information.

Printed in the United States of America
Corporate Graphics

CONTENTS

Riders aren't strapped into waterslides.

What Are Water Parks?

Water parks have waterslides. These slides are **thrill** rides. They loop. They go fast. They drop. People like going to water parks. They have fun. They get wet. They cool off. They get scared. Waterslides are like wet roller coasters. They work the same way. But they don't have seats. They don't have seat belts. They don't have tracks.

Slides like these at Aquatica, SeaWorld's water park, are called chutes.

Engineers design two types of waterslides. **Serpentine** slides have many curves. Speed slides go straight down. Waterslides have powerful pumps. Pumps push out water at the top of the slide. Riders start at the top. Engineers use water flow and **gravity** to bring riders to the bottom. Riders land in **plunge pools**.

Look!

Go to the closest water park. Look at a waterslide. How long is the slide? How steep is the slide? Are there any curves?

Stored energy is potential energy. It changes to kinetic energy.

How Does Gravity Affect Waterslides?

Waterslides use gravity's energy. They have the most energy at the top. Riders climb stairs to the top. This creates potential or stored energy. Tall slides store more energy. Riders use their stored energy throughout the ride. They go downhill. They fall. Gravity pulls the riders down. Falling builds up energy. Gravity changes stored energy into moving, or kinetic, energy.

Gravity gives riders a downward force on the Riptide Racer
at Canada's Wonderland.

Riders zip around. They follow slides. Gravity keeps them in the slides. It keeps them from falling off. It keeps the ride going.

Riders move in the direction of the ground. Gravity pushes them down. Slides push them up. This slows riders down due to **friction**.

Riders slide down slopes. The slides' **forces** are at an angle. They're not fighting gravity. This makes riders speed up.

Curves can make riders feel airborne.

How Does Inertia Work?

Engineers add curves. Curves build moving energy. Engineers design curves to make sure riders have the right amount of speed. Too much speed causes them to fly off. Riders can feel **weightless**. They don't feel as though they are being pushed down. They feel like they're in the air.

CALUMET CITY PUBLIC LIBRARY

Engineers are creating new waterslides.

Engineers must also carefully design the sides of slides. Human bodies resist changes in speed and direction. This is **inertia**. Bodies want to go straight on a slide. They try to do so. If a slide curved without sides, bodies would fly off. Instead, engineers design the sides of slides to curve up. Riders go up the sides of the slides. They do not fall off.

Ask Questions!

Ask friends if they've been to a water park. What was their favorite part? What was their least favorite part? Were they scared? Why or why not?

Bathing suits can affect friction. They rub against slides.

How Do Waterslides Reduce Friction?

Water reduces friction. It acts like oil, greasing the slide. This means riders move very quickly down a slide. They go straight down. Some waterslides reduce friction even more by using rafts, sleds, mats, or tubes. These things reduce friction between riders' bodies and slides. Riders can go even faster.

Water does the same thing roller coaster wheels do.

Water slides use **recycled** water. It's pumped from plunge pools. It's released at the top of the slide. It's also pumped through a cleaning system so that riders don't get sick. Engineers make sure there's the right amount of water. Water needs to be constantly flowing. Too much water is wasteful. Too little water is unsafe.

Think!

Think about roller coasters. How are they similar to waterslides? How are they different? Which do you like better? Why?

Try This!

Materials

foil, tape, plastic block, rubber band, ruler, sandpaper, notepad, pen or pencil

Procedures

1 Cover table with foil. Use tape to hold down edges.

2 Place block at end of table. Pull back on rubber band. Launch rubber band at block. Block should slide over foil. (Keep trying until block slides. Use less force. Use more force. Change height position of rubber band. Practice until it works.)

3 Measure how far block travels. Write it down.

4 Do this 10 times. Launch the same way. Measure distance. Write it down.

5 Figure out average distance.

6 Get rid of foil. Cover table with sandpaper. Repeat this activity.

Principle at Play

This activity shows sliding friction. It shows its effects. Objects slide differently. This is based on surface types. Friction is a force. It happens between objects. It fights against an object's motion. People push harder on rougher surfaces. This is because there's greater friction. Change surfaces. Change objects. See what happens.

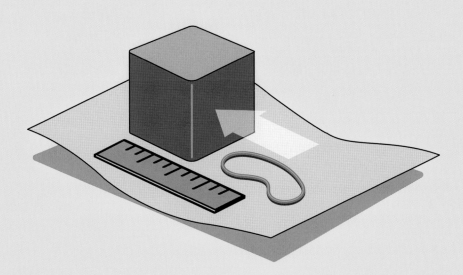

GLOSSARY

forces (FORS-iz) pushing or pulling motions

friction (FRIK-shuhn) resistance that one object encounters when moving over another

gravity (GRAV-ih-tee) force that attracts objects toward the center of the earth

inertia (ih-NUR-shuh) a law of motion that states an object stays at rest or in motion in the same straight line unless acted upon by some external force

plunge pools (PLUHNJ POOLZ) the pools of water at the end of a waterslide ride

recycled (ree-SYE-kuhld) used again

serpentine (SUR-pen-teen) having many curves, snakelike

thrill (THRIL) excitement

weightless (WATE-lis) freely falling, a feeling of not being pushed downward

FIND OUT MORE

BOOKS

Hamilton, S. L. *Water Parks*. Minneapolis: Abdo Publishing, 2015.

Masters, Nancy Robinson. *How Did They Build That? Water Park*. Ann Arbor, MI: Cherry Lake Publishing, 2011.

WEB SITES

HowStuffWorks—How Water Slides Work

http://science.howstuffworks.com/engineering/structural/water
-slide.htm
This site explains how to operate waterslides and how they're put together.

National Geographic—The Physics Behind Waterslides

http://news.nationalgeographic.com/news/2013/07/130704
-water-slide-water-park-theme-design-engineering-physics
This Web page describes the science behind waterslides.

INDEX

ABOUT THE AUTHOR

Dr. Virginia Loh-Hagan is an author, university professor, former classroom teacher, and curriculum designer. She hasn't gone swimming in over 10 years. She lives in San Diego with her very tall husband and very naughty dogs. To learn more about her, visit www.virginialoh.com.